Brave the bloodstream!

FIRST GRAPHICS
BODY SYSTEMS

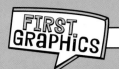

A Tour of Your Circulatory System

by Karen Ballen
illustrated by Chris B. Jones

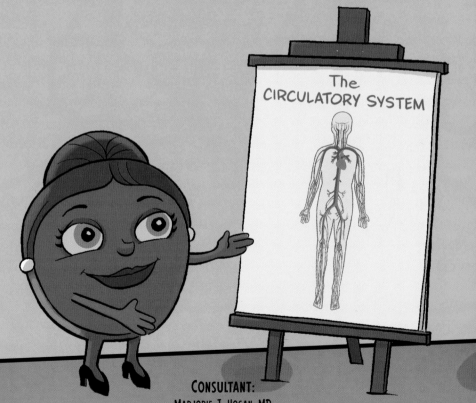

The
CIRCULATORY SYSTEM

CONSULTANT:
Marjorie J. Hogan, MD
Associate Professor of Pediatrics and Pediatrician
University of Minnesota and Hennepin County Medical Center
Minneapolis, Minnesota

CAPSTONE PRESS
a capstone imprint

First Graphics are published by Capstone Press,
1710 Roe Crest Drive, North Mankato, Minnesota 56003.
www.capstonepub.com

Library of Congress Cataloging-in-Publication Data
Ballen, Karen Gunnison.
A tour of your circulatory system / by Karen Ballen ; illustrated by Chris B. Jones.
p. cm.— (First graphics. Body systems)
Summary: "In graphic novel format, follows Ruby the red blood cell as she travels
through and explains the workings of the human circulatory system"—Provided
by publisher.
Includes bibliographical references and index.
ISBN 978-1-4296-8604-4 (library binding)
ISBN 978-1-4296-9322-6 (paperback)
ISBN 978-1-62065-261-9 (ebook PDF)
1. Cardiovascular system—Juvenile literature. 2. Blood—Circulation—Juvenile
literature. I. Jones, Chris B., ill. II. Title.

QP103.B357 2013   2011051825
612.1—dc23

Editor: Christopher L. Harbo
Designer: Lori Bye
Art Director: Nathan Gassman
Production Specialist: Kathy McColley

Printed in the United States of America in Stevens Point, Wisconsin.
032012   006678WZF12

Table of Contents

All about Blood

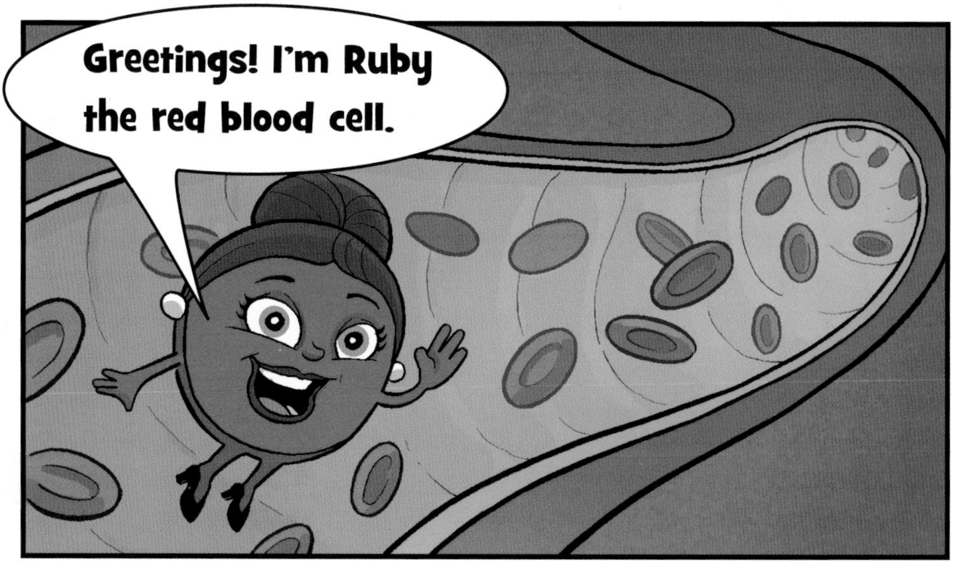
Greetings! I'm Ruby the red blood cell.

Do you know how blood moves around your body?

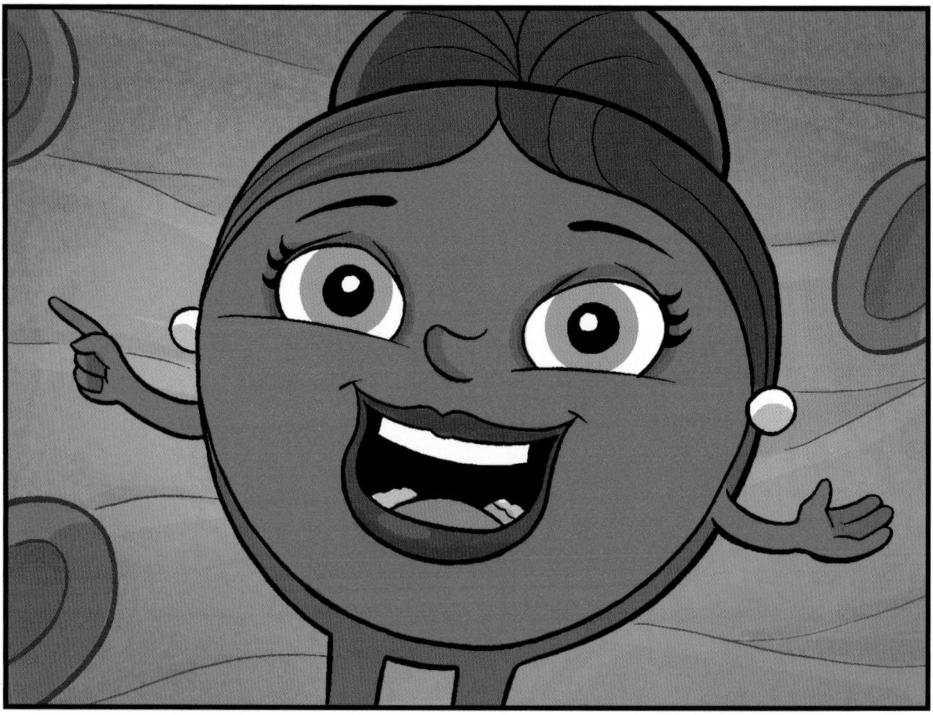

It flows through your circulatory system.

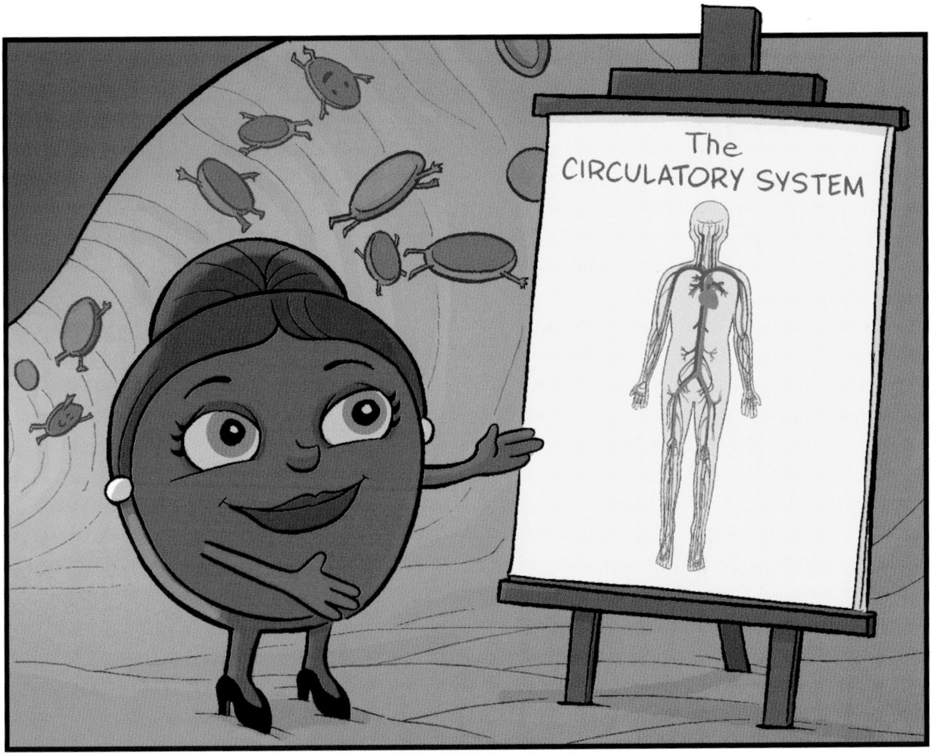
The
CIRCULATORY SYSTEM

I'm on my way to the heart.

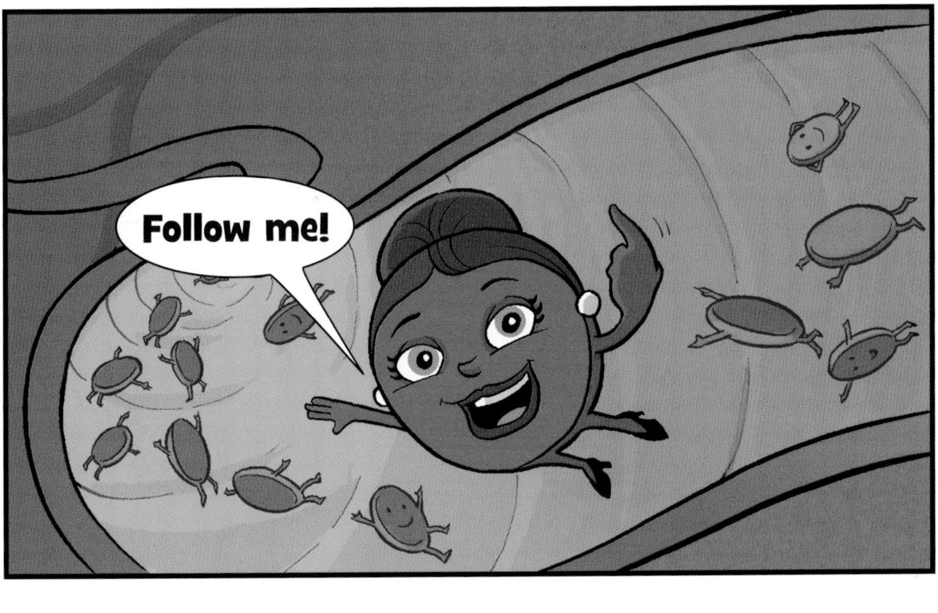
Follow me!

The heart and blood vessels are the main parts of the circulatory system.

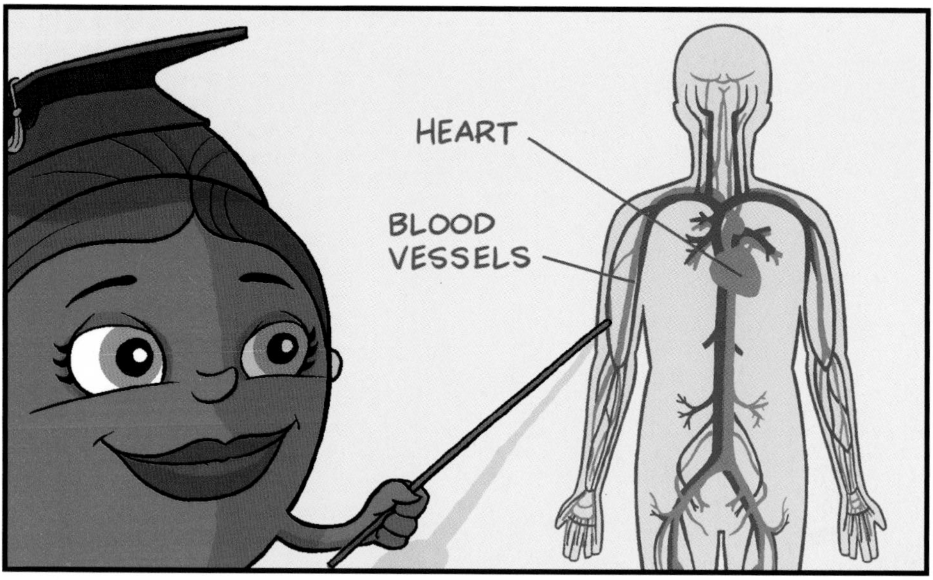
HEART
BLOOD VESSELS

The heart is a strong muscle that pumps blood.

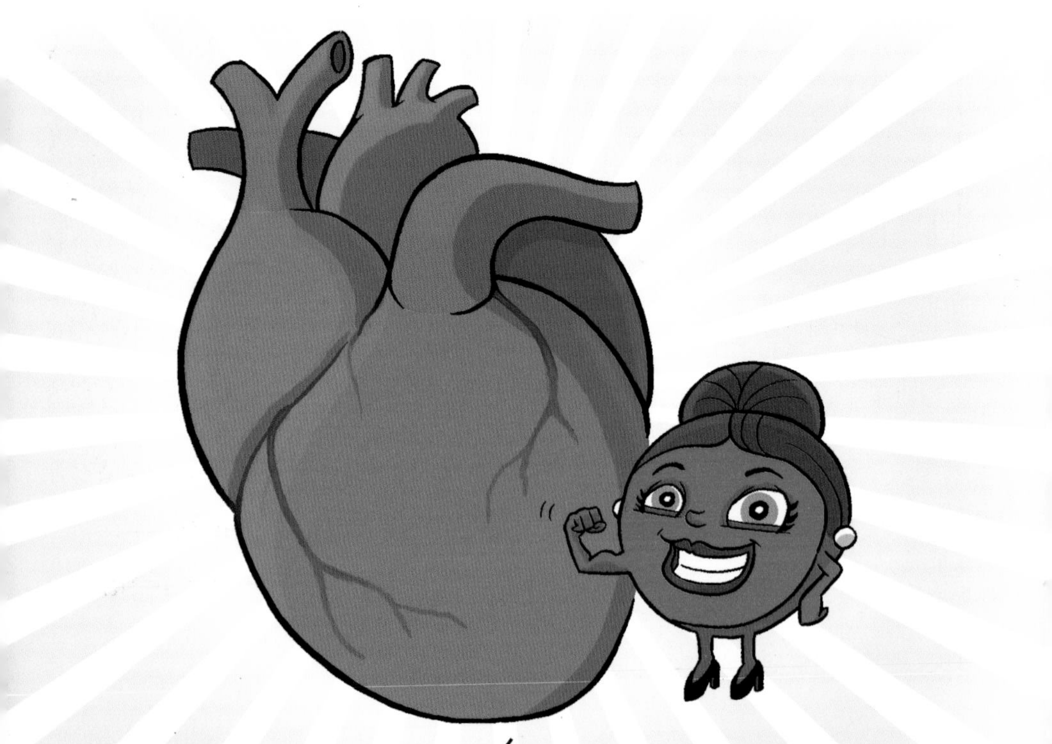

Blood vessels are long tubes.

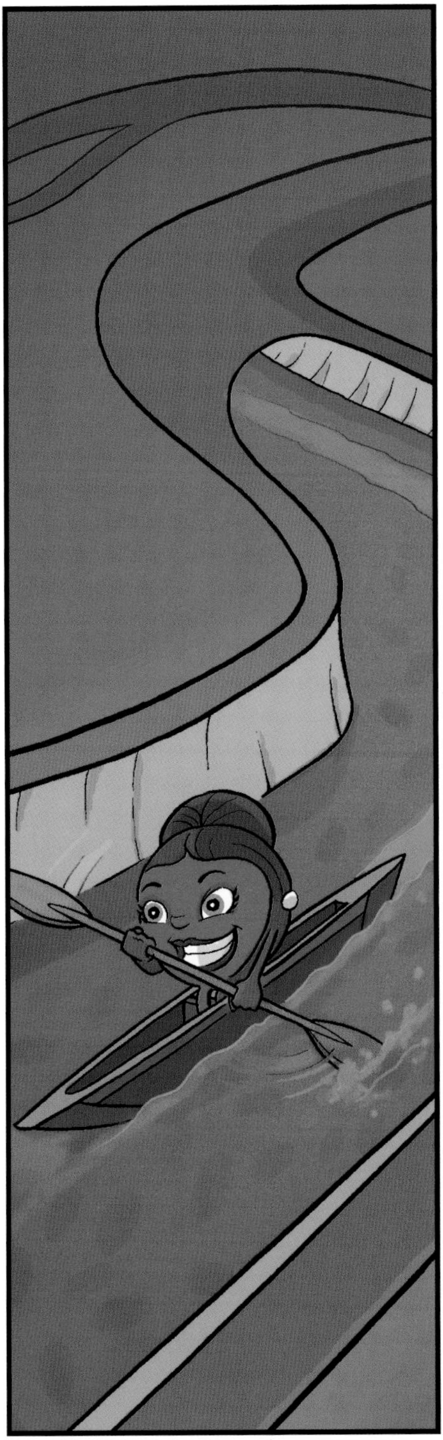

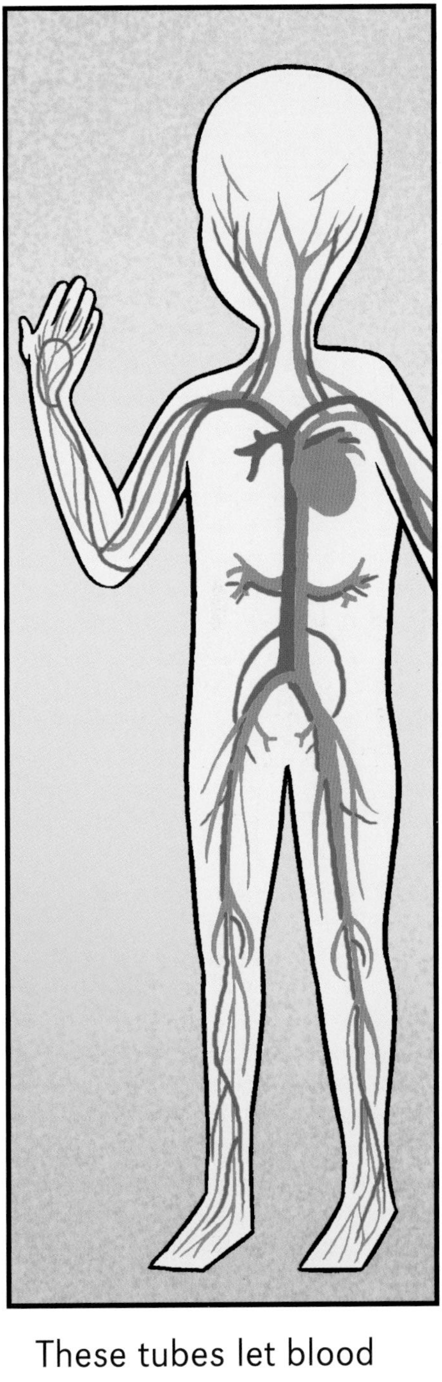

These tubes let blood flow wherever your body needs it.

And your body needs blood.

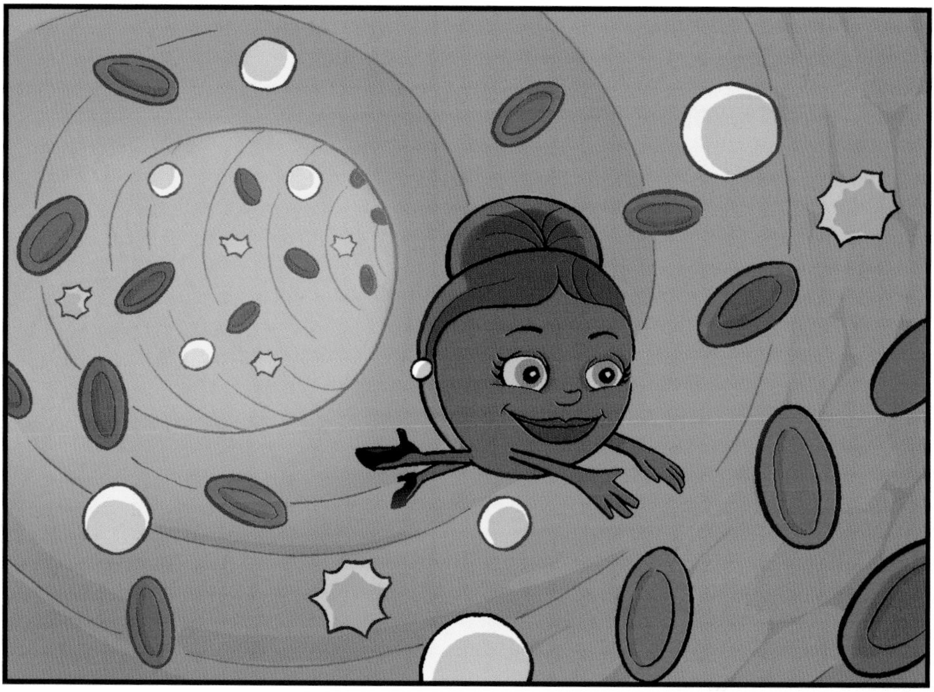

Blood brings nutrients and takes away waste.

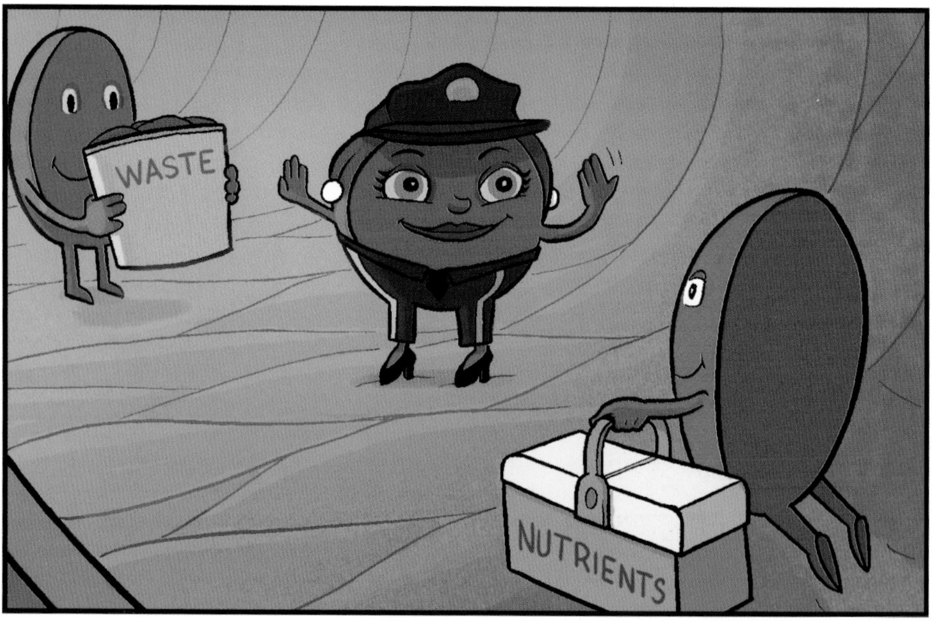
WASTE
NUTRIENTS

Blood also carries platelets and white blood cells.

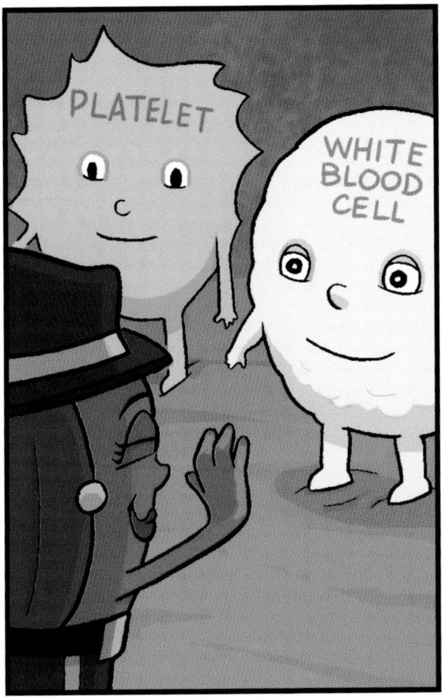
PLATELET
WHITE BLOOD CELL

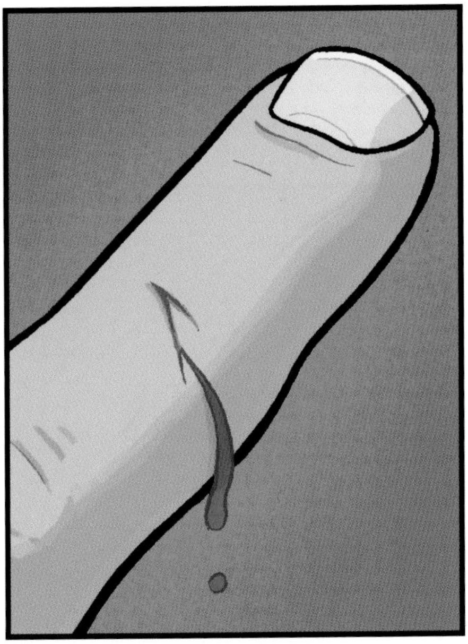

Platelets help stop bleeding.

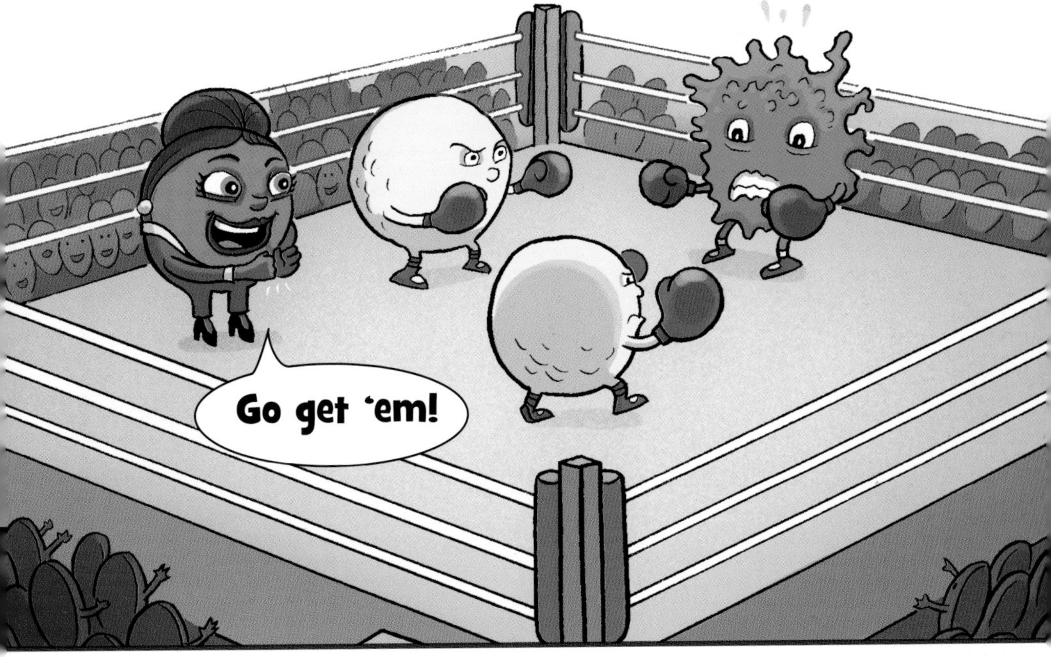
Go get 'em!

White blood cells fight germs.

I Need Air

I've reached the heart, but I won't stay long. The heart never stops pumping blood.

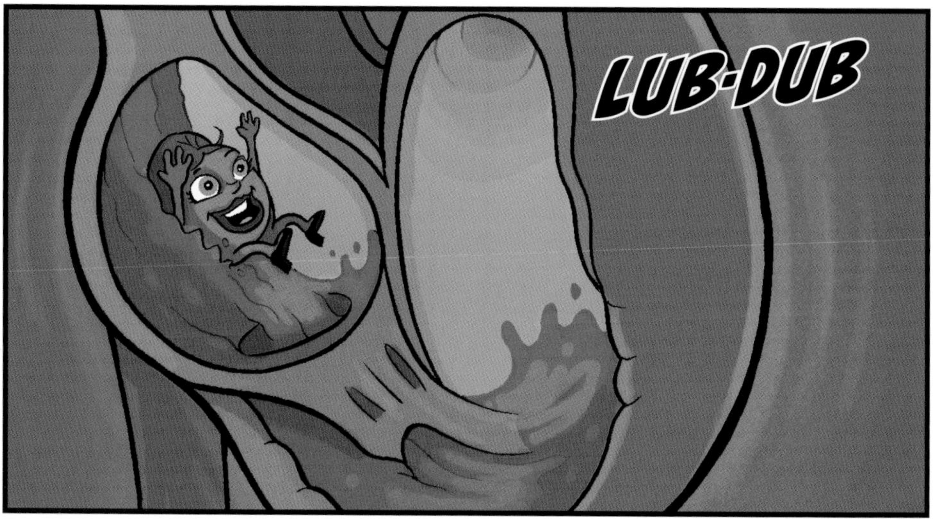
LUB-DUB

Blood coming to the heart carries carbon dioxide. This gas is a waste made by your body.

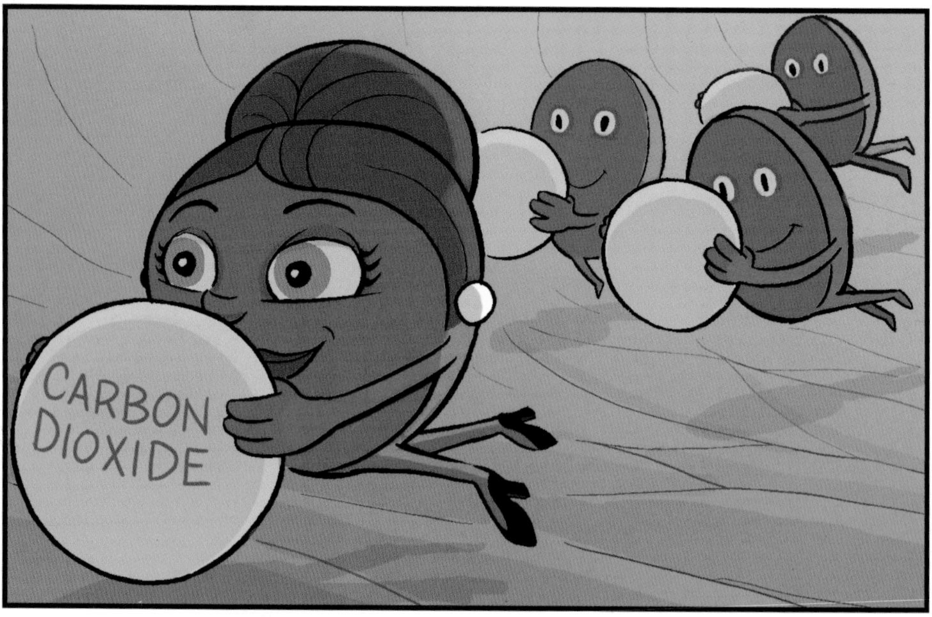
CARBON DIOXIDE

Blood takes carbon dioxide to your lungs.
Your lungs breathe out this gas.

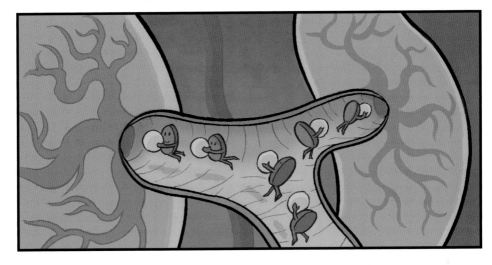

Meanwhile, your lungs breathe in oxygen.
Your blood carries the oxygen to your heart.

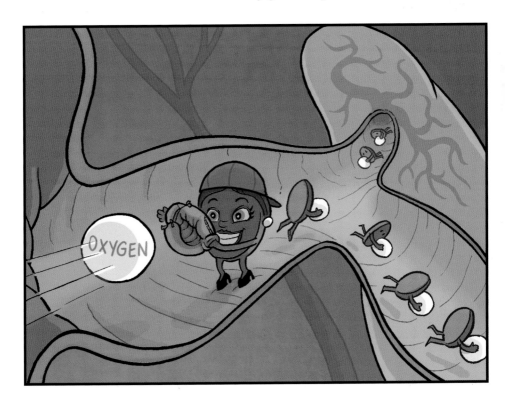

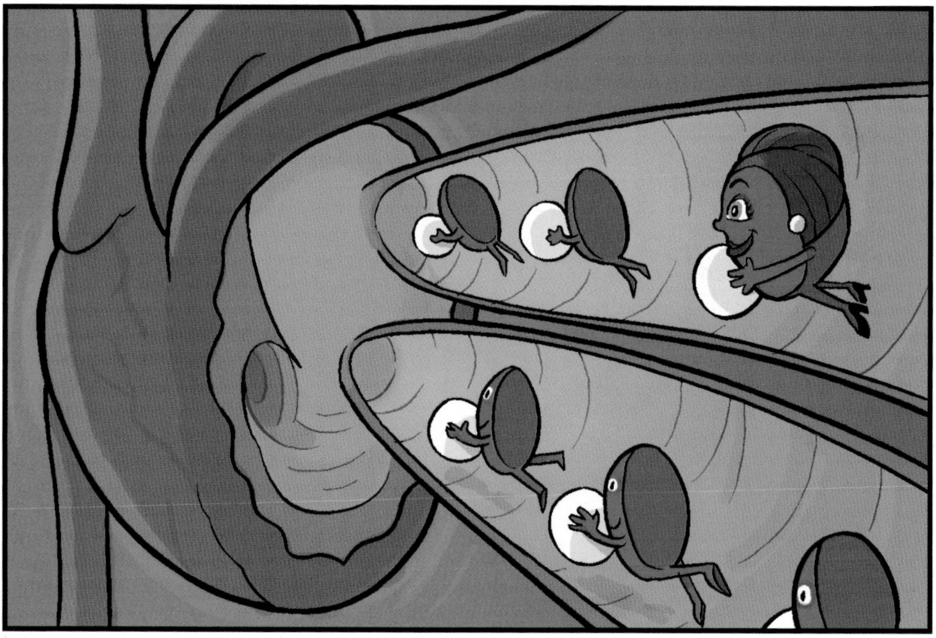

Every part of your body needs oxygen.

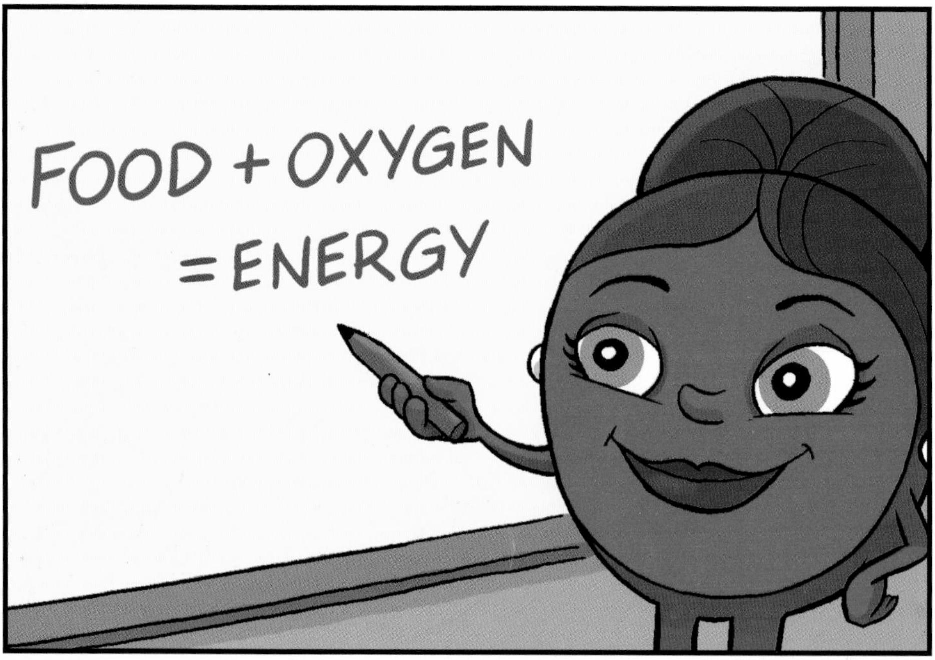
FOOD + OXYGEN
= ENERGY

Oxygen lets your body get energy from food.

Your heart pumps blood and oxygen to your digestive system, muscles, brain, and kidneys.

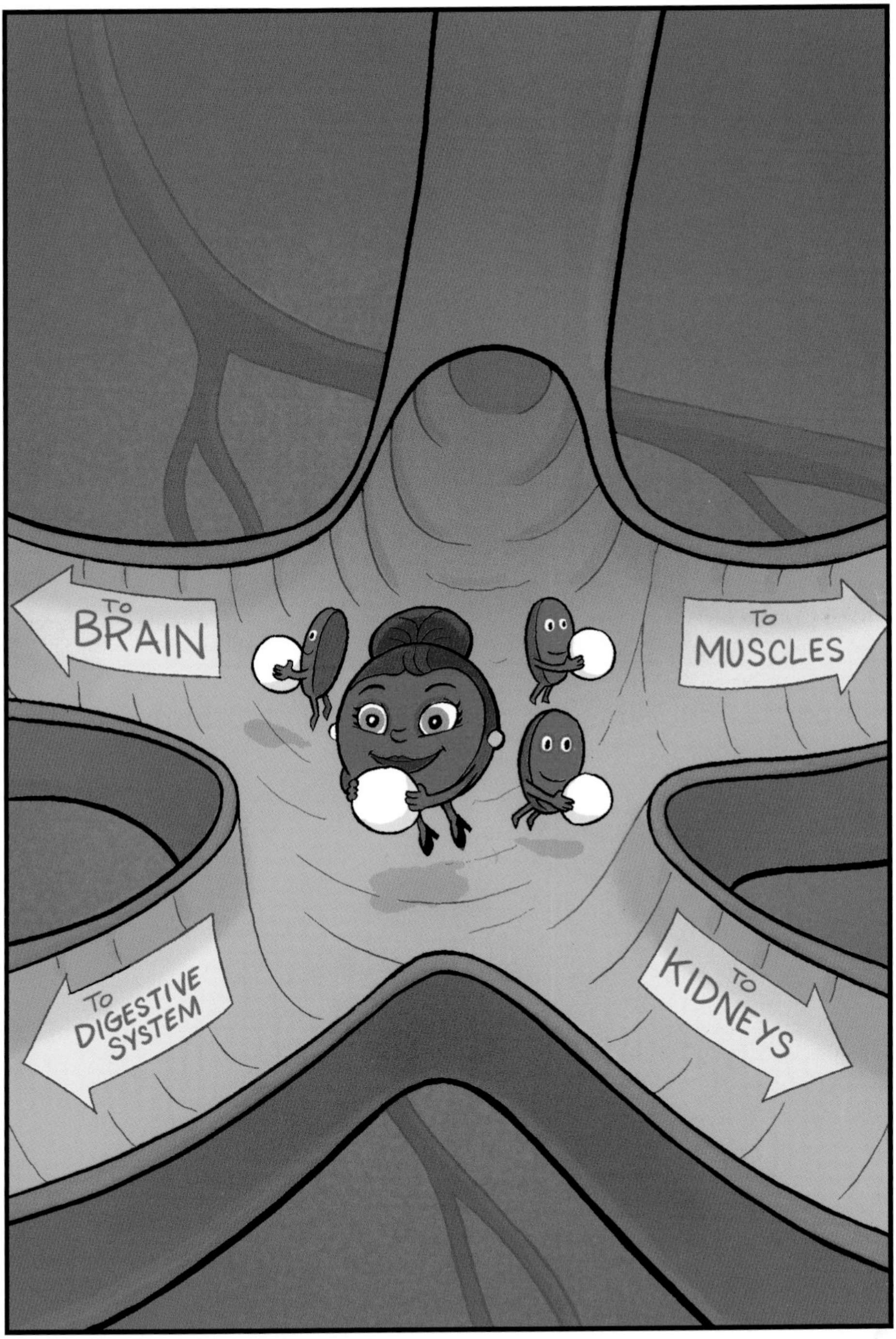

TO BRAIN
TO MUSCLES
TO DIGESTIVE SYSTEM
TO KIDNEYS

Go with the Flow

Blood goes to your digestive system to pick up nutrients from food.

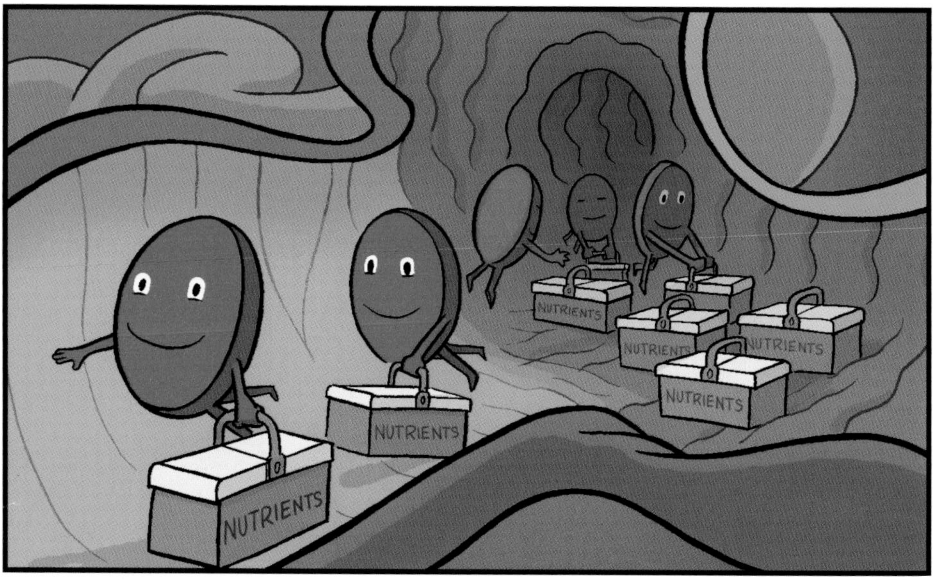
NUTRIENTS

It carries nutrients to all the parts of your body.

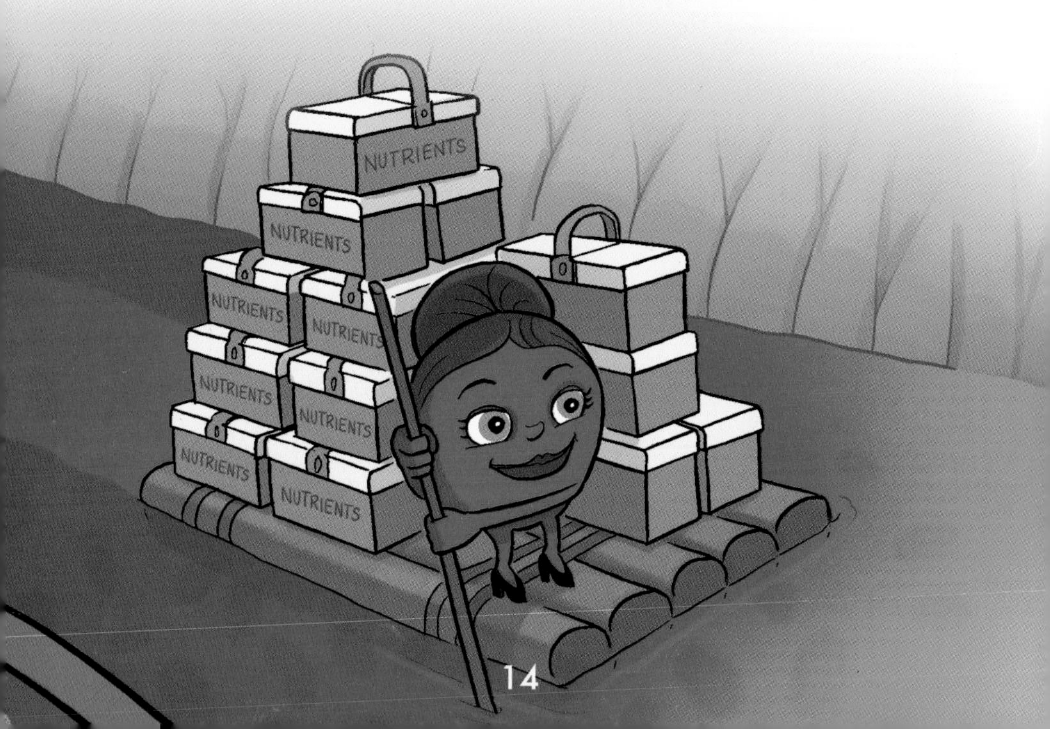
NUTRIENTS

Blood takes nutrients and wastes to the liver. Wastes include old blood cells and other things that your body doesn't need.

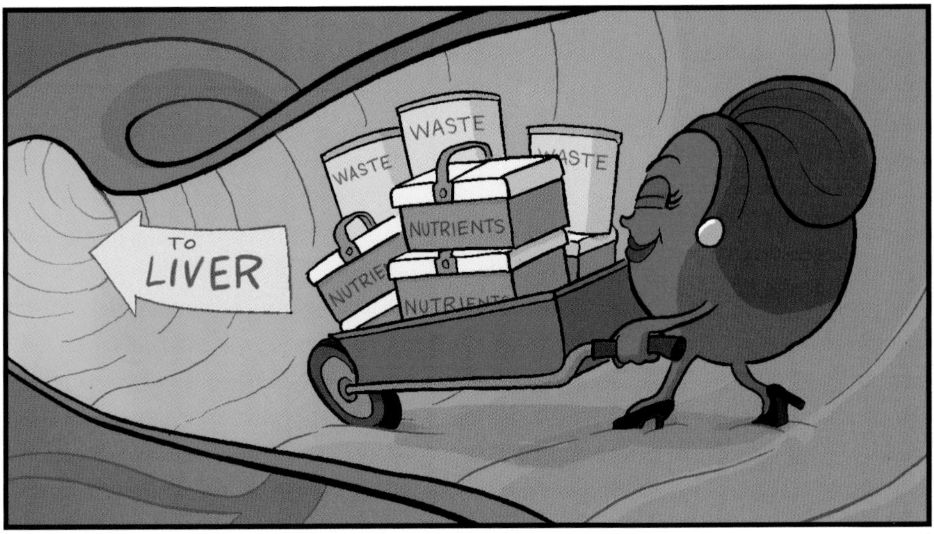
WASTE
WASTE
WASTE
NUTRIENTS
TO
LIVER

Blood picks up other nutrients and wastes from the liver. It takes food and wastes to other parts of your body.

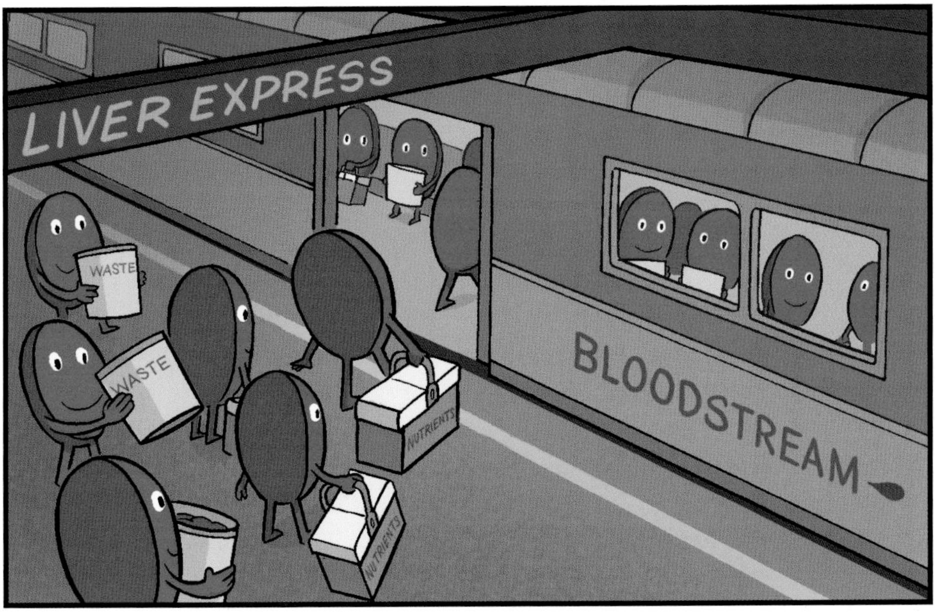
LIVER EXPRESS
WASTE
WASTE
NUTRIENTS
NUTRIENTS
BLOODSTREAM

Blood brings nutrients and oxygen to your muscles and brain.

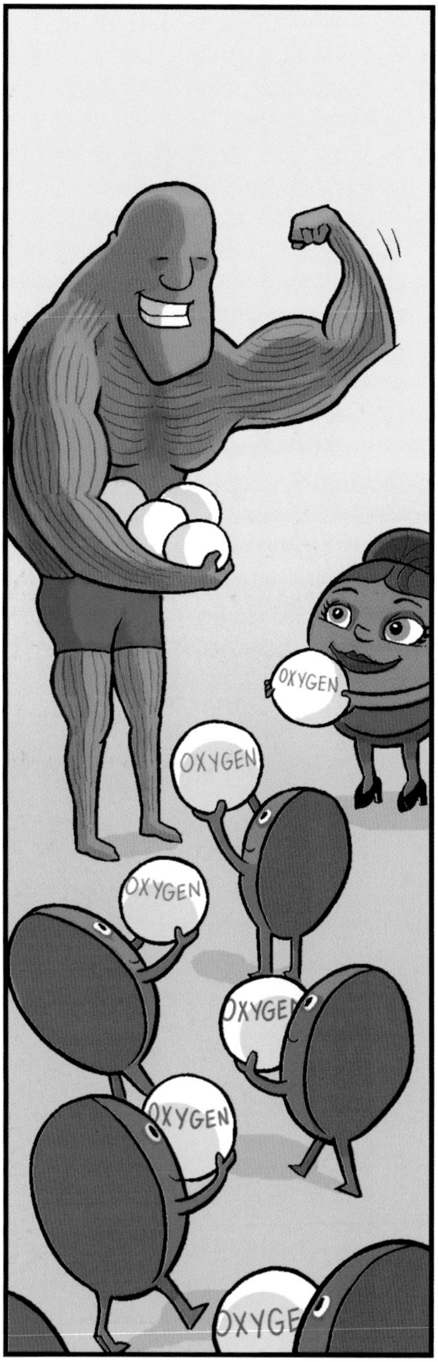
OXYGEN
OXYGEN
OXYGEN

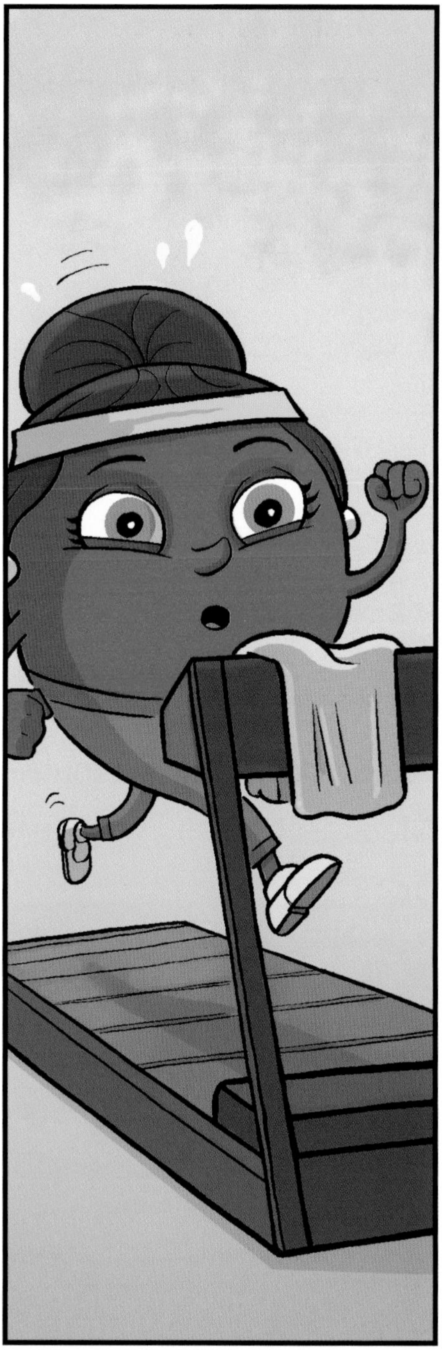

Your muscles need energy and oxygen so you can move.

Your brain needs energy and oxygen for reading, writing, and doing math.

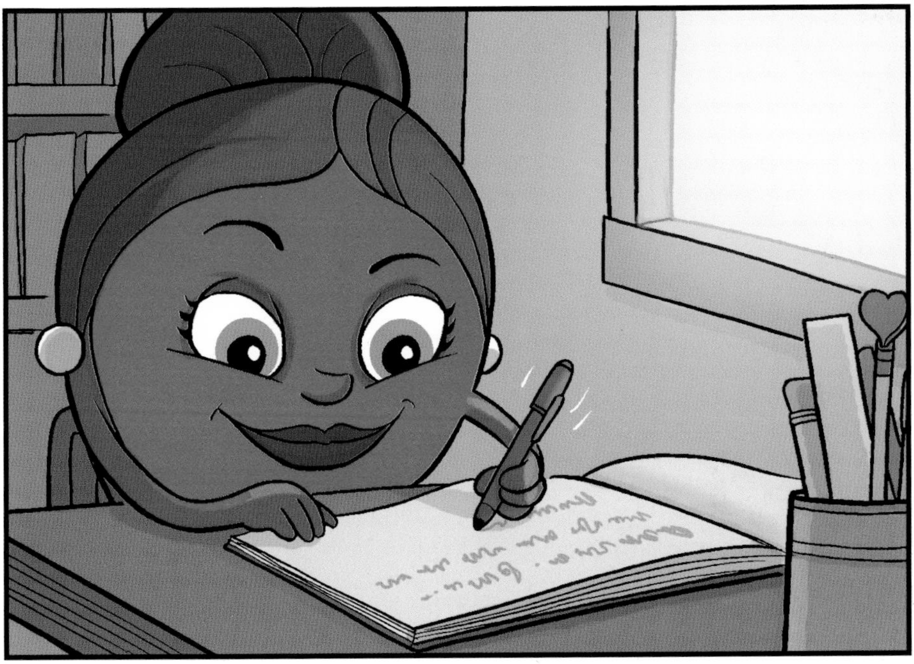

Meanwhile, your muscles and brain make carbon dioxide and other wastes. Blood carries these wastes away too.

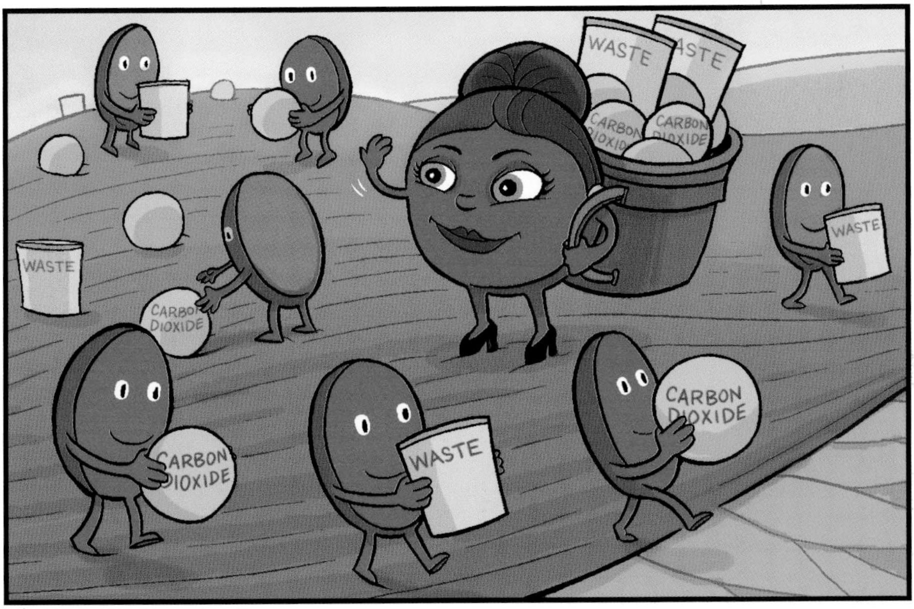
WASTE
WASTE
CARBON DIOXIDE
WASTE
WASTE
CARBON DIOXIDE
WASTE
CARBON DIOXIDE

Your blood takes some wastes to your kidneys.

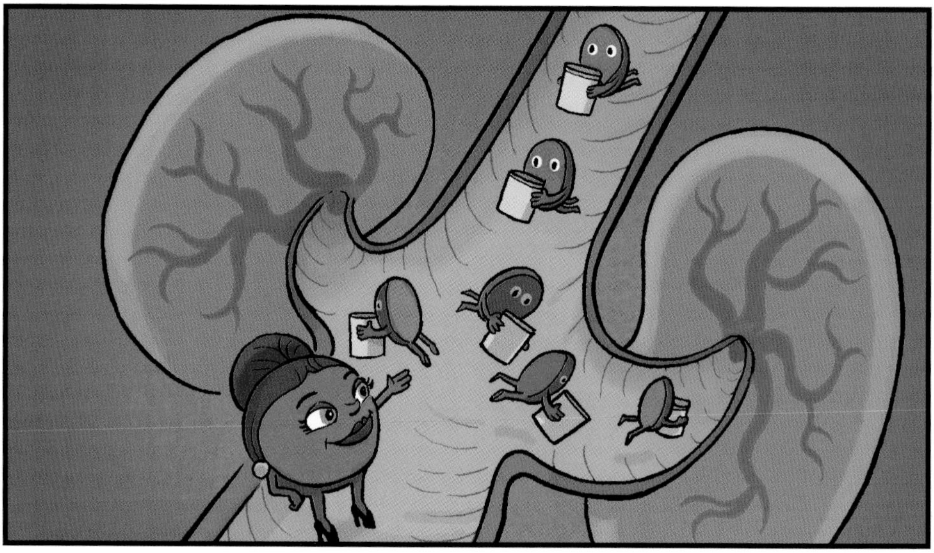

Your body makes water when it breaks down food.
Blood carries this extra water.

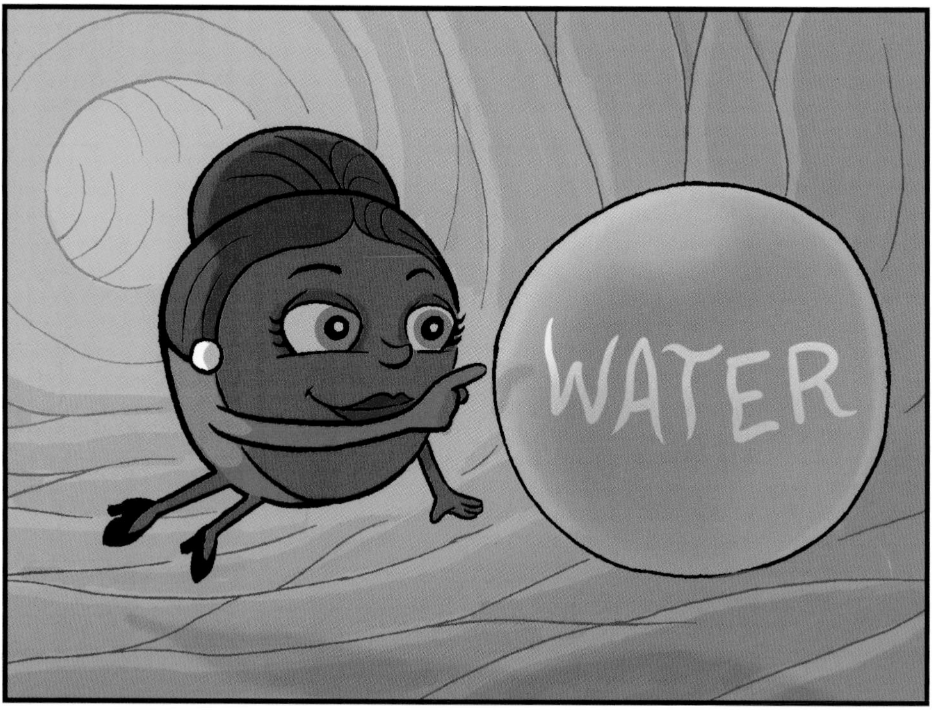
WATER

Water moves into your kidneys too.

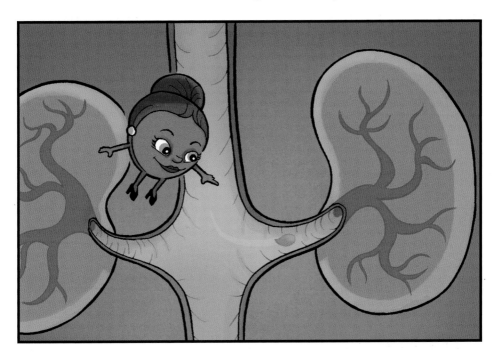

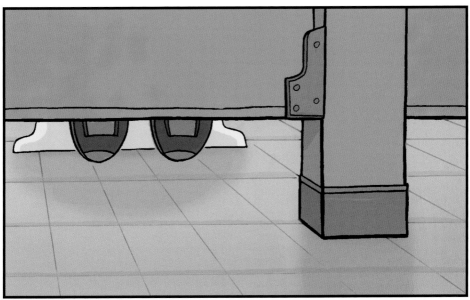

When you use the bathroom, you get rid of the wastes and water.

Around Again

After traveling through the body, blood returns to the heart.

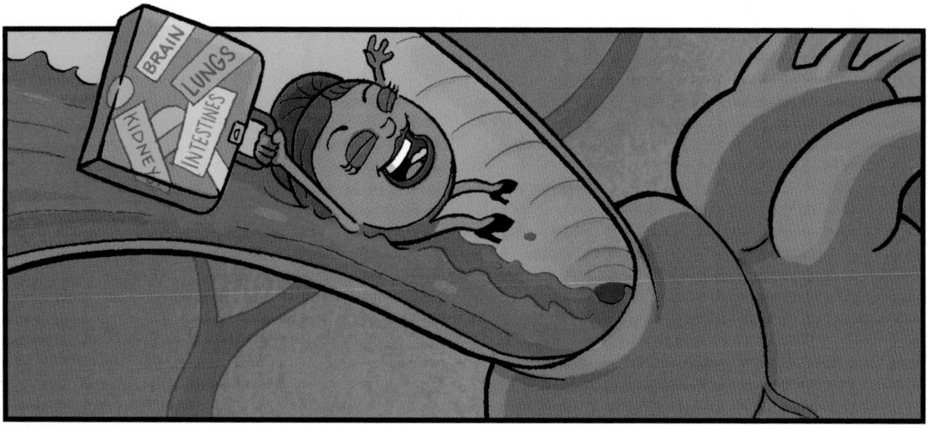
BRAIN
LUNGS
INTESTINES
KIDNEY

The heart pumps the blood back to the lungs.

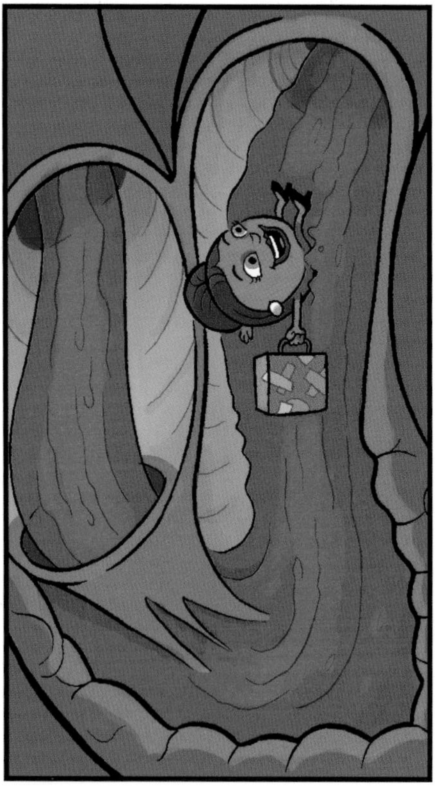

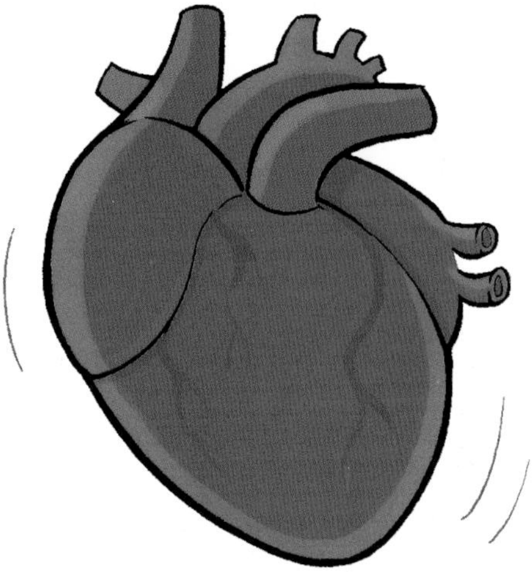

Your heart beats again and again. Your blood keeps moving through your body.

The circulatory system helps your body stay strong and healthy.

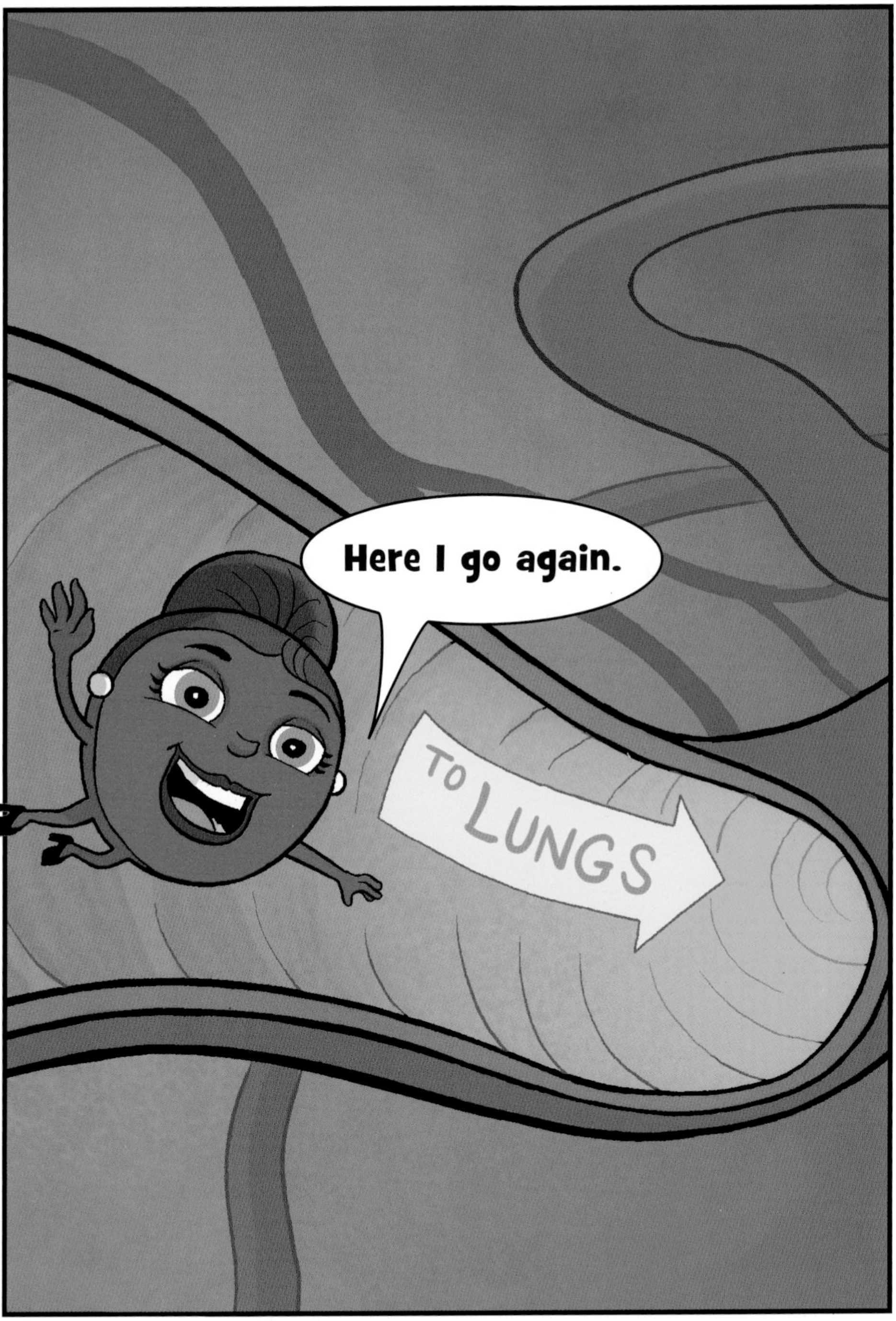
Here I go again.
TO LUNGS

Glossary

blood vessel—a narrow tube that carries blood through your body

carbon dioxide—a colorless, odorless gas that people and animals breathe out

cell—a basic part of an animal or plant that is too small to see without a microscope

digestive system—the group of organs that turn food into energy and get rid of waste

kidney—an organ that filters waste products from the blood and turns them into urine

nutrient—parts of food, such as vitamins, that are used for growth

oxygen—a colorless gas that people breathe

platelet—a tiny, flat body in the blood that helps the blood clot

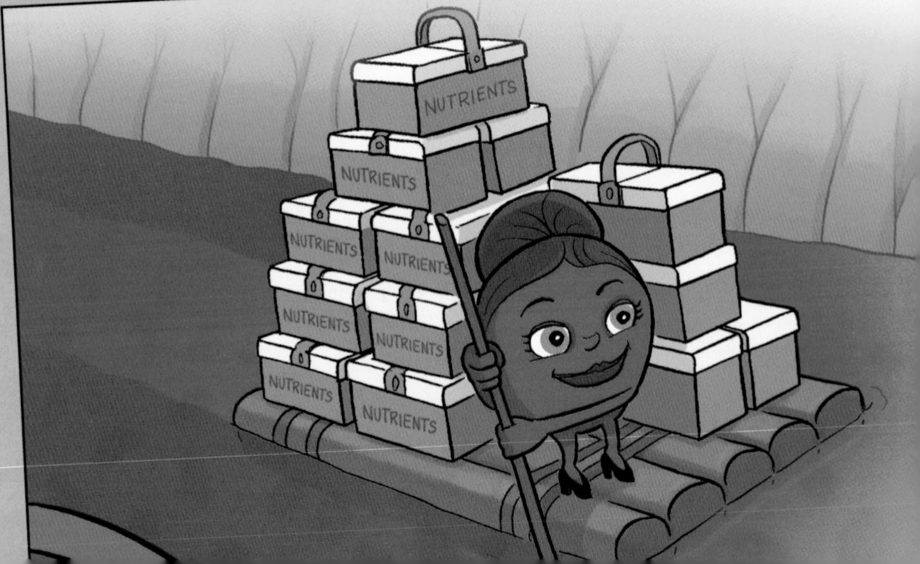
NUTRIENTS
NUTRIENTS
NUTRIENTS
NUTRIENTS
NUTRIENTS
NUTRIENTS
NUTRIENTS
NUTRIENTS
NUTRIENTS

Read More

Jordan, Apple. *My Heart and Blood.* My Body. New York: Marshall Cavendish Benchmark, 2012.

Leigh, Autumn. *The Circulatory System.* The Human Body. New York: Gareth Stevens Pub., 2012.

Storad, Conrad J. *Your Circulatory System.* How Does Your Body Work? Minneapolis: Lerner Publications Co., 2013.

Tieck, Sarah. *Circulatory System.* Body Systems. Edina, Minn.: ABDO Pub., 2011.

Internet Sites

FactHound offers a safe, fun way to find Internet sites related to this book. All of the sites on FactHound have been researched by our staff.

Here's all you do:

Visit *www.facthound.com*

Type in this code: 9781429686044

Check out projects, games and lots more at
www.capstonekids.com

23

Index

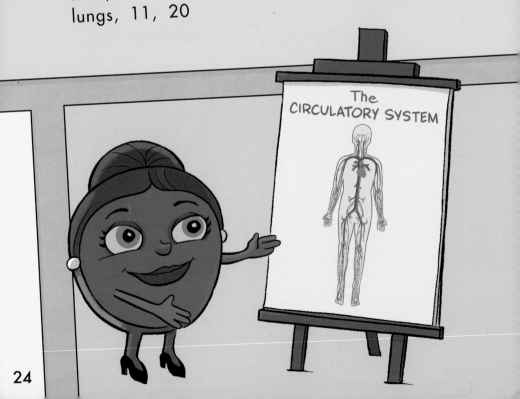

The CIRCULATORY SYSTEM

Titles in this set:

A Tour of Your
Circulatory System

A Tour of Your
Digestive System

A Tour of Your
Muscular and Skeletal Systems

A Tour of Your
Nervous System

A Tour of Your
Respiratory System

FIRST GRAPHICS

The
CIRCULATORY SYSTEM

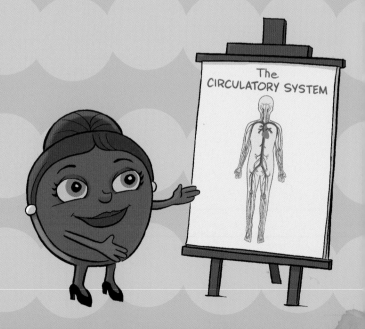